Super Gross Germ Projects

Jessie Alkire

Consulting Editor, Diane Craig, M.A./Reading Specialist

Super Sandcastle

An Imprint of Abdo Publishing
abdobooks.com

ABDOBOOKS.COM

Published by Abdo Publishing, a division of ABDO, PO Box 398166, Minneapolis, Minnesota 55439.
Copyright © 2019 by Abdo Consulting Group, Inc. International copyrights reserved in all countries.
No part of this book may be reproduced in any form without written permission from the publisher.
Super SandCastle™ is a trademark and logo of Abdo Publishing.

Printed in the United States of America, North Mankato, Minnesota

102018
012019

THIS BOOK CONTAINS
RECYCLED MATERIALS

Design and Production: Mighty Media, Inc.
Editor: Megan Borgert-Spaniol
Cover Photographs: Mighty Media, Inc.; Shutterstock
Interior Photographs: iStockphoto; Mighty Media, Inc.; Shutterstock

The following manufacturers/names appearing in this book are trademarks: AdTech™, Fleischmann's®,
Gedney®, Jell-O®, Kemps®, Market Pantry®, Morton®, Pyrex®, Red Star® Quick-Rise™

Library of Congress Control Number: 2018948858

Publisher's Cataloging-in-Publication Data
Names: Alkire, Jessie, author.
Title: Super gross germ projects / by Jessie Alkire.
Description: Minneapolis, Minnesota : Abdo Publishing, 2019 | Series: Super
    simple super gross science
Identifiers: ISBN 9781532117312 (lib. bdg.) | ISBN 9781532170171 (ebook)
Subjects: LCSH: Microorganisms--Juvenile literature. | Germs--Juvenile
    literature. | Science--Methodology--Juvenile literature. | Science--
    Experiments--Juvenile literature.
Classification: DDC 507.8--dc23

Super SandCastle™ books are created by a team of professional educators, reading specialists, and content developers around five essential components—phonemic awareness, phonics, vocabulary, text comprehension, and fluency—to assist young readers as they develop reading skills and strategies and increase their general knowledge. All books are written, reviewed, and leveled for guided reading and early reading intervention programs for use in shared, guided, and independent reading and writing activities to support a balanced approach to literacy instruction.

TO ADULT HELPERS

The projects in this title are fun and simple. There are just a few things to remember to keep kids safe. Some projects require the use of sharp or hot objects. Also, kids may be using messy materials such as glue or oil. Make sure they protect their clothes and work surfaces. Review the projects before starting, and be ready to assist when necessary.

KEY SYMBOLS

Watch for these warning symbols in this book. Here is what they mean.

HOT!
You will be working with something hot. Get help!

SHARP!
You will be working with a sharp object. Get help!

CONTENTS

SUPER GROSS!

There are tons of super gross things in the world. These things can make you feel **disgust**. But did you know this feeling can keep you safe? It stops you from touching or eating things that might be harmful.

Disgusting things can still be fun to think about. That's why many people are **fascinated** by gross things. And germs can be especially gross!

GROSS GERMS

Germs are tiny living organisms. They cannot be seen without a microscope. Did you know your toothbrush holds millions of germs? Their small size and great quantity are part of why germs are so gross.

Some germs cause illness if they enter your body. But you won't know if these germs are inside your body until you get sick!

ALL ABOUT GERMS

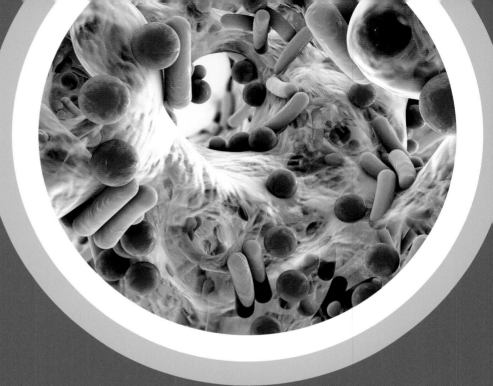

Bacteria, viruses, and molds are all types of germs. These organisms behave in different ways. They also affect humans in various ways.

BACTERIA

Bacteria are living things that have just one cell. Many bacteria live off of **nutrients** found in human bodies! Some bacteria cause human illnesses, such as strep throat. Other bacteria are good for you. They help your body break down food.

VIRUSES

Viruses rely on other living things to survive. They reproduce in the cells of people, animals, and even plants. If a virus enters your body, it can reproduce quickly. This causes illnesses, such as the flu.

MOLDS

Molds are types of fungi, which are plantlike organisms. They often grow on spoiled food. Molds can also grow in **damp** areas. They can be harmful to humans if eaten or breathed in.

MATERIALS

WHEAT BREAD

MILK

JELL-O

YEAST

APPLES

CHENILLE STEMS

NON-LATEX GLOVES

BEADS

COTTON SWABS

ORANGES

PIPETTE

PORTOBELLO MUSHROOM

FRESH SPINACH

PETRI DISHES WITH AND WITHOUT AGAR

SALT

TENNIS BALL

TEST TUBES AND TEST TUBE RACK

VEGETABLE OIL

SMALL FUNNEL

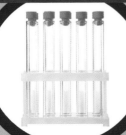

VINEGAR

MOLDY BREAD EXPERIMENT

CLEAN

DIRTY

CONTROL

MATERIALS

- three sealable plastic bags
- marker
- non-latex gloves
- three slices of wheat bread
- hand soap

1. Label one plastic bag "control." Label the second bag "dirty." Label the third bag "clean."

2. Put on the gloves. Place a slice of bread into the "control" bag and seal the bag. Take off the gloves.

3. Touch everyday items with your hands, such as shoes, phones, and doorknobs. Then take a second slice of bread and wipe your hands all over it. Place it into the "dirty" bag and seal the bag.

4. Wash your hands well with warm water and soap. Touch the bread with your clean, dry hands. Then place it into the "clean" bag and seal the bag.

5. Leave the three bags in a cool, dry place for several days. Check the bread slices each day to observe how they change.

11

ROTTING TEST

Discover how delicious food can turn gross in a matter of days with this rotting test!

MATERIALS

- four test tubes with stoppers
- test tube rack
- orange
- cutting board
- sharp knife
- apple
- fresh spinach
- small funnel
- milk

1 Place four test tubes into the test tube rack.

2 Peel the orange. Have an adult help cut several pieces off the orange. Place them into a test tube.

3 Have an adult help cut several pieces off the apple. Place them into another test tube.

4 Tear some spinach leaves into small pieces. Place the pieces into the third test tube.

5 Stick the stem of the funnel into the fourth test tube. Fill the test tube halfway with milk.

6 Seal the test tubes and let them sit for several days. Observe them each day. How long does it take each food to start rotting?

13

APPLE DECOMPOSITION

Experiment with different **substances** to see how they affect apple pieces as they rot!

salt

Oil

Vinegar

air

MATERIALS

- four plastic cups
- marker
- measuring cup
- water
- salt
- spoon
- vinegar
- vegetable oil
- apple
- cutting board
- sharp knife

1 Label each plastic cup with the name of the **substance** going into it. There should be a cup for salt, oil, vinegar, and air.

2 Stir salt into ¾ cup of hot water until no more salt will **dissolve**. This liquid will go into the "salt" cup.

3 Fill each cup about halfway with the correct liquid. Leave the "air" cup as is.

4 Have an adult help cut an apple into even slices. Add an apple slice to each cup. Then place the cups somewhere out of the way.

5 Observe the apples for up to two weeks. The saltwater should dry out the apple. The vinegar should kill bacteria. These factors should best prevent rotting.

BUILD A GERM FARM

Grow bacteria to make your own germ farm!

Labels on petri dishes: Keyboard, door handle, Shoe, phone, dog mouth, toilet, counter, human mouth, faucet, mouse

MATERIALS

- items to swab
- petri dishes with agar
- marker
- cotton swabs
- bottled water
- tape
- tray
- paper
- pencil

1. Think of surfaces or items that could have a lot of germs. Examples include a kitchen counter, toilet seat, cell phone, door handle, keyboard, and refrigerator handle.

2. Label each petri dish lid with the name of the surface or item you want to swab.

3. Take a cotton swab. Make sure not to touch the cotton on the swab.

4. Wet one end of the swab with bottled water.

5. Rub the wet end of the swab on the surface or item.

Continued on the next page.

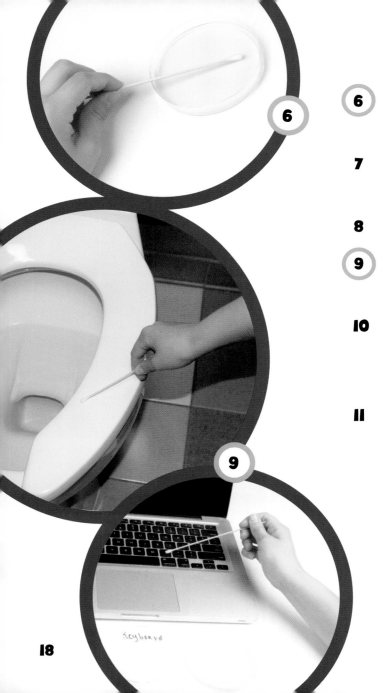

6. Rub the same end of the swab on the **agar** of the matching petri dish.

7. Place the lid onto the petri dish. Tape it closed.

8. Throw away the used cotton swab.

9. Repeat steps 3 through 8 with the rest of the items you want to swab.

10. Place the petri dishes onto a tray. Place the tray in a warm room where it is out of the way.

11. Observe your petri dishes for two to three weeks. Sketch what the dishes look like each day. How long does it take for bacteria to grow? Which item had the most germs?

Grossed Out!

The more often you use an item or surface, the more likely it's covered in germs! This is also true for items and surfaces shared by many people. These include countertops, computer keyboards, and toilet seats. Washing your hands before and after touching these items helps prevent the spread of germs!

FLU VIRUS MODEL

Make your own model of a flu virus!

MATERIALS

- tennis ball
- craft knife
- chenille stems
- pencil
- ruler
- scissors
- hot glue
- beads

1. Have an adult use a craft knife to cut a half-circle opening in the tennis ball.

2. Twist a chenille stem tightly around a pencil.

3. Pull the chenille stem off the pencil. The chenille stem should be a curly coil.

4. Repeat steps 2 and 3 with more chenille stems.

5. Fill the inside of the tennis ball with the coiled chenille stems.

6. Cut another color of chenille stems into several 2-inch (5 cm) pieces.

7. Bend the end of one chenille stem piece so it forms a right angle.

Continued on the next page.

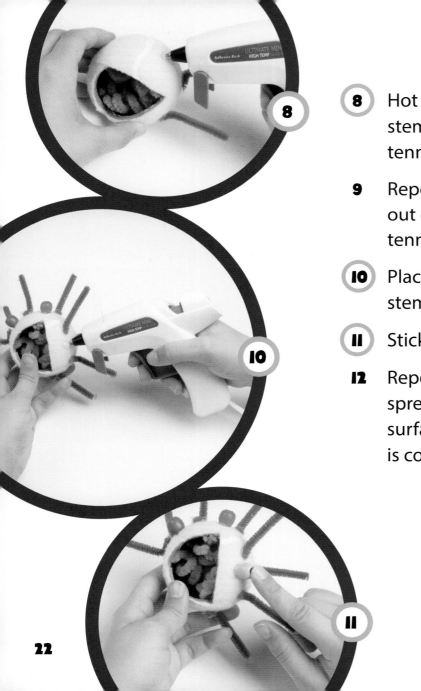

8 Hot glue the short end of the angled chenille stem piece onto the outside surface of the tennis ball.

9 Repeat steps 7 and 8 so the stems are spread out evenly around the outside surface of the tennis ball.

10 Place a small glob of hot glue near a chenille stem spike.

11 Stick a bead onto the glob of hot glue.

12 Repeat steps 10 and 11 so the beads are spread out evenly around the outside surface of the tennis ball. Your virus model is complete!

Grossed Out!

Flu viruses spread quickly. They attach to cells in the human body. **Protein** spikes on the outside of the viruses help them attach. These spikes are commonly called H and N spikes. After attaching to human cells, viruses **release** genetic material called RNA into the cells. This is how the viruses reproduce!

STRUCTURE OF A FLU VIRUS

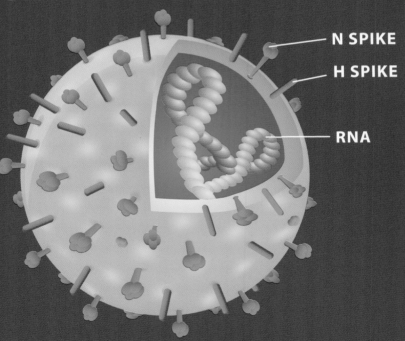

N SPIKE

H SPIKE

RNA

EDIBLE BACTERIA

24

MATERIALS ⬤

- water
- measuring cup
- large bowl and spoon
- 3-ounce box of Jell-O powder
- pitcher
- petri dishes
- tray
- pencil and paper
- small food items such as candies and licorice

1 Have an adult boil 1 cup of water.

2 Pour the water into the bowl. Stir in the Jell-O powder until it **dissolves** completely.

3 Add 1 cup of cold water. Stir to combine.

4 Pour the Jell-O mixture into a pitcher.

5 Carefully pour the Jell-O mixture into the petri dishes. Fill each petri dish about halfway.

6 Place the petri dishes onto a tray and put the tray into the refrigerator. Let the Jell-O refrigerate for three hours or until nearly set.

Continued on the next page.

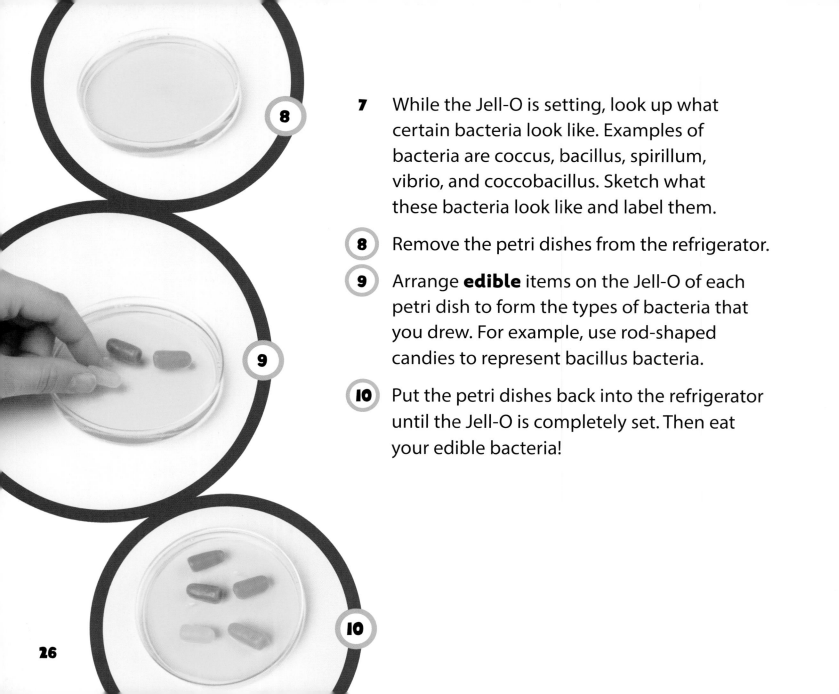

7 While the Jell-O is setting, look up what certain bacteria look like. Examples of bacteria are coccus, bacillus, spirillum, vibrio, and coccobacillus. Sketch what these bacteria look like and label them.

8 Remove the petri dishes from the refrigerator.

9 Arrange **edible** items on the Jell-O of each petri dish to form the types of bacteria that you drew. For example, use rod-shaped candies to represent bacillus bacteria.

10 Put the petri dishes back into the refrigerator until the Jell-O is completely set. Then eat your edible bacteria!

Grossed Out!

Bacteria are usually one of three different shapes. Spherical or coccus bacteria are circular balls. Rod or bacillus bacteria look like rounded rectangles. Spiral bacteria are curved or twisted.

SHAPES OF BACTERIA

COCCUS

SPIRAL

BACILLUS

MUSHROOM SPORE PRINT

Use a big mushroom to make a fungus **spore** print!

MATERIALS

- portobello mushroom
- cutting board
- sharp knife
- white card stock
- water
- pipette
- empty bowl
- hair spray (optional)

1. Have an adult slice off the bottom of the stem and lower part of the mushroom so its folded gills are exposed.

2. Place the mushroom onto the card stock with the gills facing down.

3. Use the **pipette** to drip a few drops of water onto the top of the mushroom.

4. Cover the mushroom with a bowl overnight.

5. Remove the bowl the next day. Lift the mushroom carefully. It should leave a print on the card stock. This print is from **spores** that dropped from the underside of the mushroom. Spray the spore print with hair spray if you'd like to preserve it!

FUNGUS FRUIT BREAKDOWN

See how fast an orange breaks down with yeast, a type of fungus!

MATERIALS

- two sealable plastic bags
- marker
- orange
- cutting board
- sharp knife
- yeast

1   Label one bag "control" and the other "yeast."

2   Have an adult help cut the orange in half.

3   Put one orange half into the "control" bag. Seal the bag.

4   Place the other orange half onto the cutting board so the fruit's flesh faces up. Cover the flesh of the orange with yeast.

5   Put the orange half into the "yeast" bag. Seal the bag.

6   Let the orange halves sit in a warm area for a few days. The orange in the "yeast" bag should decompose faster. This is because fungi **release proteins** that break down food.

GLOSSARY

agar – a jellylike substance used as a base for growing living organisms for scientific study.

damp – slightly wet.

disgust – a strong feeling of dislike toward something unpleasant or offensive. Something that gives the feeling of disgust is described as disgusting.

dissolve – to become part of a liquid.

edible – safe to eat.

fascinate – to interest or charm.

nutrient – something that helps living things grow. Vitamins, minerals, and proteins are nutrients.

pipette – a narrow tube used to suck in and push out small amounts of liquid.

protein – a substance found in all plant and animal cells.

release – to set free or let go.

spherical – relating to a sphere. A sphere is a solid figure that is round, such as a ball or a globe, and has every point the same distance from the center.

spiral – a pattern that winds in a circle.

spore – a seedlike cell made by some plants.

substance – anything that takes up space, such as a solid object or a liquid.